CW01647483

Servant of Time

Poetry Collection

THERESA JONES

First Published in 2020

by AboutTime4T Publishing

Copyright & Related Rights Act 2000. These moral rights are the paternity right of Theresa Jones to be identified as the author of the book titled Servant of Time,

the integrity right (the right to prevent mutilation, distortion or other derogatory alteration of the work) and the right of false attribution. No part of this book and eBook may be copied or used without prior consent of the Author.

All rights reserved. No part of this publication may be reproduced, stored in a retrieval system or by any means, electronic, mechanical, photocopying, recording or otherwise without the prior written permission of the author, or as expressly permitted by law, or under terms.

Images by: Pat Burns (patburns59@icloud.com)

You must not circulate this book in any other binding or cover and you must impose this same condition on any acquirer.

Copyright © 2020 Theresa Jones

All rights reserved.

Paperback ISBN: 978-1-8382943-0-4
eBook ISBN: 978-1-8382943-1-1

About this book

This poetry collection paints a portrait of life, one women's journey told
through poems that reflect the reality of many women.
To shine a ray of hope.

It is told in four sections.
People & Life, cancer, dementia, suicide;
family lost, taken before their time as in *Months Mind, White Roses, I Wander.*
Grief laid bare as a table set for others to dine on.

Nature Heals, a mindful journey through the Comeragh Mountains
in *Bagwell's Folly, Around Clonmel, Apples* and others.
The wild isolation of the *Nanny Water Cottage* in Laytown.
How the environment restores our sanity in *Footsteps* and reduces stress
through the call of the blackbird, rushing water of a mountain stream,
rustle of leaves on trees in the wind or crunch beneath our feet in *Autumn.*
A balm for the soul.

Relationships, the resilience of women, the support others give or not in
Walls, Gilded Cage, Street Angel – House Devil.
The possibility of restoring self-esteem to endure life's challenges,
slay your dragons, calm your anxiety;
then as a phoenix rise to rebuild your life and value your skills.

Observations and Memories is an ironic look at how people treat
each other and the environment. To know that T*rue Friends* will tell you
if your knickers are showing or lipstick is smudged.
In *Remember Me*, a look at local politicians and how they network.

A poetry collection to remind us that strangers can often treat us better
than we treat ourselves until we learn to love the stranger within.

Acknowledgements

I am very lucky to belong to local writing groups with a fabulous group of talented writers who support, inspire and motivate the writer within.

A big thank you to

Margaret O'Brien of Poetry Plus, Brewery Lane Theatre, Carrick-on-Suir, a wonderful host of real and virtual meetings. Margaret's collaboration with Linda Fahey of the Tudor Artisan Hub affords writers many opportunities to work with musicians and artists on local projects such as the Clancy Festival, Carrick-on-Suir.

My local Tipperary Libraries:
Attended held by Clonmel Library with Margaret Galvin; who encouraged Bernie Condon, Joe Whelan and myself be the Backroom Poets.
Clonmel library played host to the Backroom Poets on Culture Night 2019.
Maura Barrett of Cashel Library for her creative writing workshops & literary evenings. They are a great support.

Huge thanks for the fabulous support needed for this book:
Eileen Acheson,
a wonderful poet and friend, who gave endless advice.
She is the author of the wonderful poetry collection
"*I Wonder*".

Joyce Murphy, author of "*Inner Rumblings*" and
Neil Dennehy, author of "*What to do with Stardust*".

Pat Burns, photographer based in Co. Meath; for the beautiful photographs.
Storm Brendan, 2019, Laytown, Co. Meath (Cover)
Nanny Water Cottage, Laytown, Co. Meath (Nature Heals)
Derelict House, Co. Cavan (Relationships)

And lastly,
Bernie Condon, my fellow Backroom Poet and writer,
who believes in me more than I do myself.
A great friend and support during these strange times.

Dedications

For my parents, who loved a good verse.

Contents

Contents

People & Life

These things are sent to try us

Servant of Time

The cloak of the Reaper brushes the earth.
Death is a stowaway,
it goes away
but comes back another day.

Collecting souls.
Harvesting some,
rejecting others
whose hourglass holds sand still to be used.

A subtle rebuke for a gift not valued,
while many worthy of life battle
to hold on to the mortal coil.
Claimed too early,
subject to the Grim Reaper's scythe.

He is not judge or jury
but a farmer reaping his crop.
Souls released from one life
to await rebirth in another.

Not judge nor jury.
He is not to blame.
Just a servant of time
when the hourglass is empty.

Inheritance

In six-inch heels you walked an Irish mile.
Click, clack, over Snipe Hill.
As industrious as knitting needles,
lethal as an assassin's blade.

Up and down over hills of tarmac
to a cottage with an acre;
you wished to claim.

Thin as a needle, dressed to the nines,
sharp eyed; silver tongued.
You whisper, befriend, beguile.

Cigarettes nestled next to
pillar box red lipstick.
Secrets kept safe,
under the clasp of your handbag.

Thin lips pursed drawing smoke,
open to tempt the long-kept secret.
Prod and poke.
Poison dripped into the ear as vodka is poured.

Pretense of sympathy,
soft words, a soothing poultice.
Draw sad tales, unburden her tired heart.

Trouble brewed; family history stirred.
You sought a wedge to divide.
Careless of hearts broken or sides taken,
to gain a legacy you were unable to grasp.

Fortnight Lord

From council house mouse
to country estate lord,
he set off from London's Euston Station
boarded the ferry train.

Battered brown suitcase
held closed by cracking leather belt.
Gripped tightly on the rolling Irish ferry.

He unpacked under faded roses
in a boyhood bedroom, a returning hero,
made good across the water.

Tall tales to be told,
while Guinness settles
and Paddy is poured.

Served in Campbells bar;
behind one of three doors
quietly placed between the undertakers and the grocery.

In town, he reigns supreme,
drinks all round.
Taxi back out the road, delivers him in style.

The brothers hold their tongue, they pass no remarks.
Keep the welcome.
The big **I am** is home.
All hail the fortnight Lord.

Tea Leaves

Grandma read tea leaves.
The future stuck to the bottom
of your bone china cup.

Indistinct black patterns
laying bare your
secrets or desires.

A family expert on hand.
No need to cross palm with silver.
Be ready, discover what your life may hold.

Tales of roads to be travelled.
Steps to be taken
with strangers you are yet to meet.

Sip your tea, drain the cup
to almost the bottom.
Swirl around, your destiny awaits.

Gin

Darkened room, heavy red curtains
drawn mid-afternoon.
Packet of polos reflected in a glass of lime,
concealing gin beside the bed.

Bronchial cough
wearies the lungs,
smoking to ease
the passing of time.

Memories haunt the night.
Heavy the nicotine fog.
Mills & Boons pages turn.
150 pages, another doomed romance.

Sweet stories drip poison into a still romantic soul.
Validates, the reality of loves lost
or heartaches born.

Children raised in ignorance.
Until as adults they ask hard questions.
Break the silence.

Bridget or Pat

Let me naturalise you. What's your name?
Bridget, Biddy.
We have enough Bridget's here.
You can be Pat.

Pat became your name until the end.
Over forty years. London war time years.
Fear and Suspicion.

Don't disagree. Just fit in.
Disagreements could lead to isolation.
Who are you really?

A shrug, why wouldn't you be a Pat?
Take away who you are. Take your identity.
Your past. Your land.

Or move away. Reinvent. Begin again.
Did you care?
Pat in England; Bridget in Ireland.

You became who you wished to be.
A change of name.
Insult or an opportunity?

Who are you really?
The answer, whoever you prefer to be.
Pat or Bridget.

Let it be your choice.
For so many,
their name may be all they have left.

White Roses

On the last day I brought you white roses in bud.
The nurses found you a jar, a run on vases.
Cancer is a busy ward.

Moved to a room
on your own.
Never a good sign.

White roses in bud.
Hospital heat drained life from the bouquet.
You were fading. The roses were fading.

From bud to full bloom.
When the last petal fell
it took your soul with it.

Dad

Maurice Jones was a careful man.
Careful with money, it was hard to come by.
Careful with words, they were easily spent.

A wry sense of humour.
Called my best friend 'mid-day'.
He said she would never be up for Dawn,
unless we were late home!

Driving me to school, he found daily humour
when passing our Unigate milkman.
Parked, waiting at the gates of West Norwood Cemetery.
9am deliveries for the dead.

When the bookies were raided,
armed men locked the regulars in.
Waved a shotgun while tills were emptied,
called for everyone to sit on the floor.

No, Dad told them, 'bad back and bad knees.'
He leant heavily on his blackthorn walking stick.
Face resigned, even way bet clutched.
Rare winnings to be collected.

5 pence each way. The daily gamble.
Dog 2 and 3 reversed had romped home.
Poor Dad, a winner and a loser.

Front row seat obtained. Sympathies won over.
Winning slip pocketed for the next day.
Maurice Jones sat. A rare story to be told.

Uncle Albert

A master baker, when there were such things.
Knew how the dough was made;
just by touching the bread.

Taught me how to swim in the Adriatic Sea.
Splashing in armbands under a hot Italian sun.
Golden sands and ice creams,
always a smile and kind word.

A stroke stole him away, in a time
when state institutions were called mental homes.
They housed the remains of the lost souls
whose brains could not control their bodies.

For years on Saturdays, we climbed
steep green iron stairs to visit Albert.
Lost amongst a sea of beds where others were drowning alone.
No-one to save them or remember who they once were.

Just Another Day

My Mother misdiagnosed;
too respectful to question.
Left at the end in a public ward
curtains open to stew on a commode.

Ravaged body, needle loose from the drip.
Wrists dripping with blood as raw meat.
Grey head bowed, too weary for complaint.

Young nurses gathered around a station.
Laughing, drinking tea.
A break from a procession of patients.
Just another day.

So many years later.
Do these nurses need the care of others?
Lives come full circle.

For some young nurse,
learning her trade,
are they too
just another day?

Almost made the Telegram

One of nine siblings, almost all lived long lives.
Except George, who died in the War to end all wars.

A strong woman equal to her challenges through two world wars.
Forthright, she did not mince her words, her wit was legendary.
She would not queue for the ladies, having seen it all.

At the end, Grandma lay in hospital, almost 100.
She could not stop smiling, unlike her really.
A man's teeth forced between aging gums, her own apparently lost.
She almost made the Queen's telegram.

The Funeral

Dad died after evening visiting hours.
A phone call, a young nurse untrained for such events.
Please return quickly, then added there was no rush.

Funeral delayed by a month to a grave diggers strike.
Weary mourners waited in cars for a busy Priest.
Altar boy swung incense enthusiastically until the first two rows choked.

Dash from Catford to West Norwood Cemetery,
more waiting.
The priest lost on unfamiliar one-way systems.

Grave diggers emptied mugs when the prayers ended.
Shovels poised, earth dripping, mourners weeping beside them.
I issued an invitation to join my parents, if they wished.
Sullen yellow jackets slunk back to JCB.

During funeral tea, the community minibus called.
He's been out already. I rang last week.
Retreating driver tutted, consulted his list.
We buried him today. Shake of the head, I'll make a note.

Months pass, many letters to sent back and forth.
Chasing hospital and doctors equipment. Long returned.
Years pass. Hip operation scheduled. Cancelled.

So many letters received, calls made.
Dad would have enjoyed the irony that
he received more attention dead, than alive.

Victorian Duchess

I was raised in South West London in a grand Victorian house,
above the underground River Effra on Christchurch Road.
The busy South Circular. London's artery road.

I was raised by wartime ethics and Victorian values.
We recycled before it was fashionable.
Used washing machines as cat beds.
Never discarded what could be used.

My mother made bread pudding.
Mix stale breadcrumbs, sultanas,
almonds, demerara sugar, orange peel long soaked
in dark Jamaica rum. Pressed down then sliced.
Mouthfuls of heaven as sultanas pop.

My grandma believed that children that were seen
but not heard. We all read; it was a house of books.
Hardbacks and paperbacks stacked everywhere.
Classics with Westerns. Pig Farming with Poetry.
Mills & Boon, Dickens.

The dark basement sitting room,
waited all day for the sun,
only to close the curtains to see the televisions.
One for picture, one for sound.

Pantry shelves were filled with Sloe Gin,
pickled horseradish, preserves.

Huge rusty printing press,
only resident in damp musty cellar.
Omnipresent, silent. Served its time.

First floor, lean out of the sash windows,
hang washing on the line,
be careful of the 30 ft drop.
Peg it down well.
100ft of line, best drying in London.

Long garden lined with majestic trees
with wide gaps where Dutch Elm disease struck.
Deep raised beds overflowed with runner beans and marrows;
but never carrots, Dad said the trees took all the good.

Last time I passed there were cobwebs on cobwebs,
cracked windows, torn net curtains.
Down on her luck.
A discarded Victorian duchess that drank heat like port wine.

Wartime Stories

Saturday afternoons, stories were told.
My parents and grandmother reminisced about the war.
Memories of bombs, shortages, blackmarket, wartime songs.

They sung Pack up your Troubles;
and as I thought, My body lies over the Ocean.
I was enthralled, ears wagging, open book on lap.
Placed in a corner with orange squash and rich tea biscuit.

My favourite were stories of Probyn Road,
where my parents rented a top floor flat.
Raised chickens in the attic under a bare bulb.
Wrung their necks when they reached an age for the table.
Bodies dancing about the floor, unaware of their demise.

A conker tree lost a large limb during a bombing raid.
Garden wall smashed to smithereens.
The old ladies in the ground floor dragged the limb inch by inch
through the back door to burn in the kitchen grate.

Each night at half past eight, they locked the garden gate.
Walked back along the dark path strewn with bricks.
Backdoor wedged open, the branch was covered by the heavy blackout
curtain until at last it was fully consumed.

Broken Child

A broken child within, will demand your attention.
It needs some space, some peace of mind.
Broken child is your lifelong companion.
Crying and pulling at your pockets.

At the altar, it said, "We are not ready".
"We are not sure". You did not listen.
Tugging at the veil that covered your eyes, your true vision.
Each time things went wrong, this child clamoured to be heard.

Reminders of hiding in a wardrobe, muffled shouting, fear.
Suffocating in furs, struggling to breathe.
Gazing into glassy eyes of long dead fox heads.
Or ice skates on a bedroom door. Naive innocence stolen.
Fear, confusion, mocking laughter. Shame followed in its wake.

This child was neglected, you journeyed on alone, created distance.
In quiet times, it caught up. Stalked you in your dreams.
You ran, became someone else, a charade.
This was not you; you were not whole.

Your underlying fault was exploited, vulnerability became blame.
Look side by side in the mirror. Child and adult.
Together yet estranged. No love lost.
Two halves sharing one soul. Reconcile to journey forward.

The adult must heal, love the child;
Assign no fault. There is no profit in blame.
Swallow the bitter pill.
Forgiveness faces you in the mirror.

Do not abandon the child.
Embrace wholeness. Throw open your heart.
Continue the journey together as one.

Metal Fillings

Dr Bacon's practice was a ten minute
walk up my road. A large Victorian house
converted into a dental practice.
Nothing modern about either.

The dark waiting room had a
large fish tank filled with green water,
behind which was a picture of dinosaurs.
I was sure he had monsters.

The dentist's room had the same high windows.
6 ft high to a plaster corniced ceiling.
Covered with secondary double glazing.
Yellowed by age and in need of a good clean.

Dr Bacon was to fill my five-year-old mouth
with dark metal. Weak teeth, he said.
An injection was administered, no nurse.
He leaned over, flared nostrils and
deep concentrated breathing.

He returned later; anaesthetic long gone.
I must have moved while he drilled.
He hit the gum, blood spurting, he investigated
pressing his big thumb, which I bit and ran.

I was returned, chastised by my Mother
extolling his virtues. This is the man
that saved your brother's teeth.
Saved them where?
I thought, looking at the fish tank monsters.

Under the Lilacs

Blousy lilac blossoms
that reached for the clouds
bestow their sweet scent.

Stolen by a yellow warning gale.
Blossom scattered to rot on garden soil.
Heavy scent lost for another year.
Beauty taken in an evening.

Cherish what is good now.
Take opportunity without question.
For it may pass on by.
Seeking another that longs for its presence
more than you.

Where's Annie?

Annie Byrne was always quiet and sensible.
Her sisters spent their rent money on clothes,
then hid behind the sofa smothering laughter,
while the rent man knocked at the door.

Now only old songs rekindle Annie's memories.
Names to flit around her mind, elusive when grasped.
Dance as butterflies, joining names to faces long loved.

Annie is lost, travelling on a perpetual journey.
Wandering through the maze of her mind.
Her body sits, warm in a soft pink cardigan,
plaid blanket tucked across her knees.

Visiting loved ones feel sorrow,
Annie's brief moments of clarity are bittersweet.
Renewed loss, their eyes brim with unshed tears.
Sharp like sting of a nettle on a blue summer's day.

Victim of Circumstance

Latchkey boy raised on toasted Mother's Pride,
scraped with margarine barely covered in baked beans.
Father hitting double top at the White Hart.
Mother cleaning up West.

He was streetwise early, part of a gang.
Left school as he turned 16 and took the dole.
Long days to fill with havoc and destruction.
He stalked the streets for trouble and so often found it.

She was happy until the day they walked the same street.
A life of skipping ropes and roller skates.
Until that day he changed her life.

Her young life ruined, skates and skipping rope put away.
Six years before the vote and adulthood.
She became silent, sullen, changed.

He boasted to his friends, named her name.
News travels fast, her world shrank, became small.
He reveled in the cheap glory of destruction.
School bullies taunted her... whore.

Just another statistic, another unreported crime.
Society protects the latchkey boy, this under-dog.
Social workers and therapists would paint him the victim.
Absolve his guilt, victim of homelife situation, never stood a chance.

Catholic guilt stilled her tongue, no profit in telling her truth.
No words spoken could absolve that which was stolen.
She drew black eye liner to brave the world,
forever changed, seen through adult eyes.
Just another victim of circumstance.

Maturity

Hold fast to the mirror,
gaze briefly into eyes.
Reflect colours of forest glade.

Careful not to indulge.
Pity is a deep pond in which to drown.
Stand shoulder to shoulder with your inner child.
Reconciled.

Too long rejected,
divided by memory.
Made whole by the necessity of healing.

Maturity does not come with age.
You are mature
when you are and not one day before.

Suicide

Not for the first time but the last.
Finally, successful in his quest.

A car that could not be sold second hand,
remove the pipe, no-one the wiser.
Evidence now.
No more miles for this clock.

No misadventure this.
Flat field of graves,
Inconspicuous markers of passing.

Stones hardly seen,
almost embarrassed to be there.
Laid to commemorate
a life barely lived.

Avenue of the Dead

i.m. Kevin

The hearse drove slowly down
the avenue of the dead.
Endless grass over a patio of stones
that cast no shadow.
No proud markers these.

Family torn apart with grief.
Numbed emotions.
Broken hearts expand and tear.
Hollow eyes, weary from tears.

You were not laid to rest.
There were no shared stories.
No laugher in memories.
We are still raw. We still grieve.

There was no pity.
No shared condolence.
Only the shame of a life half lived.
Dreams unfulfilled.
Still ripple through time.

There is no peace.
You were not laid to rest.
We still wonder why.

Month's Mind

i.m. Nora

Swift the passing of weeks.
Then Month's Mind. **
Wave of guilt at having smiled.
Now and then.

Twice,
you have died for me.
Twice,
I have grieved your passing.
Twice,
I laid you to rest.

Once,
for your body,
Once,
for your soul.

Your memory cuts deep, my heart cracks anew.
Month's Mind reopens wounds.
Grief, an endless well.

For some, this may be healing.
For me, a reminder time has passed.
And you are gone.

**Months Mind is the Mass Service that is held in Ireland a month after a person has passed away.

To Wander

Sometimes the mind takes an unplanned journey.
Dressed up as a daydream,
to wander through the perpetual maze.
Lost to our world.

Lost to wandering, gazing upon delights, discover new wonders.
Tempting one to stray further, chasing butterflies,
Drifting with dandelions into the otherworld.
Captive in fantasy, dreaming.

At times, doors open back to this world,
Recalled by a face in a photograph
by a familiar voice that this worldly body hears
or an old song that draws it home.

All too brief, the short trip back to this body
that whiles away waiting
for the mind lost wandering.

Nature Heals

Nanny Water Cottage

Nanny Water cottage, idyllic romantic dream
of an Irish thatched cottage.
Wild, isolated;
as much of the sea as it is tenuously attached to the land.

Stands at the tidal mouth of the River Nanny since 1800s.
A river rich with trout, eel, mullet but not salmon;
it is locally said that they were banished by St Patrick.
A coast guard station set to guard against smugglers.

A sentinel facing out to sea.
Snuggles beneath brown thatch, thick white walls absorb spray.
Blue doors and windows drink in a clear view of the sea.
Surrounded with a protective cloak of boulders and rocks.

Saviour and witness in 1831 to the sinking
of the smack Wellington caught in a storm.
Laden with potatoes from Lock Ryen.

Rescuer to a cart swept away before the river had fully ebbed.
Man revived and girl saved
but not the poor horse, lost to the deep.

Spectator from 1868 to Laytown Strand races,
Dublin day-trippers, respectable sea bathers
down on the train to take the sea air.

The Nanny cottage stands proud and aloof.
Resistant to the passing of time.
A watcher on the shore.

Spring Moon

Eager to perform,
the impatient moon
tires of waiting in the wings.

Though pale,
declares its fullness
in the sky
before the sun even sets.

Glowing iridescent
in the denim blanket
of the evening sky.

Limelight is retained
not dimmed
or diminished
by the supporting cast of stars.

Only to be eclipsed
in beauty by the rising sun.
So welcome after rain filled days.

Spring awakens,
as Winter abates
and Summer seems possible,
at last.

Around Clonmel

Clonmel our vale of honey.
The grey stone arch of the West Gate rises above
to welcome festival visitors.

A gate here once stopped Cromwell and his army.
The bells of St Mary's ring out at 6pm across parish lands.
Black wrought iron gates of the Quaker cemetery
are closed to protect the friends who have passed.

Walk Church Road where bluebells and crocus cover
the secret tunnel that led the workhouse poor
to end their days in the Asylum.

On to Marlfield where St Patrick's well
will soothe your soul with solitude,
a balm to our busy lives.

Stroll the lake where ducks and swans will clamour
to be first for the bread or will nip the knuckle
if you are too slow to share.

Visit the forgotten places,
the hives among the purple rhododendrons at Kilnamack,
climb the hill to Bagwell's Folly overlooking the River Suir.

Cannon Hill, walk the Munster way to the Holy Year Cross
and on to Long Mountain.
If you dare, pass the Ireland homestead
or the ghostly Glenary Village, now just walls and memories.
A monument to the past, a green museum. Victim of progress.

Turning back head down, inhale the honeysuckle, dream to blackbird song.
Walk the dappled forest paths, throw stones in Glenary River,
listen to the running water and let your stress dissolve.

Explore Carey's Castle, where children play hide and seek in the tower.
Drift away to the mournful call of the buzzards, haunting call of the cuckoo.
See how small things are, way above the honeyed vale.

Apples

The smell would tell you it's Autumn.
All around Clonmel, the smell of apples spoiling,
awaiting The Crushing.
Piled up against the wall in Dowd's Lane.

There would be men working, who may only get work
during The Crushing. Long days spent in pulp.
A race against time, while rats raced over rotting fruit.
A harvest for all.
Cider put Clonmel on the map, the taste of Summer.

Windfall apples welcome in Autumn,
sitting deep in the pockets of returning school children.
Couples stroll down honeysuckle lanes,
say goodbye to warm Summer evenings.

These are nights for the fire.
Warm kitchens stocked with sugar and honey.
Where Mothers peel September away,
stew the fruit to sweeten the long damp Winter.

Frosty Halloween brings children and adults alike
bobbing the apple. Shiny red faces, dipping into
buckets of water. Keep your hands behind your back.
Who would be the first to bite the apple and win?

Then Christmas with its bounty, an illusion of plenty.
Followed by the long haul of Winter,
the cold and dark evenings eventually drag to Spring,
Dainty blossoms dress apple trees like a bride,
While bees hum around like bridesmaids.

Summer fruits drink up the sun and rain,
While men who only work The Crushing,
wait for the next Season to begin.

Guardians of Bagwell's Folly

Bluebells grow between forgotten stones
covered in blankets of moss.
Fallow deer peek behind old oaks,
perhaps they are waiting, watching.
Guardians of the stones of Bagwell's Folly.

The oaks have been here so long.
Spectators when Bagwell built his folly in 1814.
Placed high on a Comeragh hill,
he watched for Napoleon, who never came.

The folly remains, overlooking Cannon Hill and the River Suir.
Ghostly young deer, float through an indigo mist of bluebells,
run beneath the cloak of purple rhododendrons.
over deep green moss
that wrap the secrets of this sacred place.

Forest paths ring to childish laughter,
the guardians of the hill watch only the walkers now.
Napoleon is long gone,
a threat no-more to the oaks on the hill
shielding a rich man's folly.

Footsteps

Stomp up the hill, footsteps like thunder
beat a tattoo on the clay baked path.
Dark thoughts match gunmetal clouds.

Hauntingly slow the call of the buzzard,
chased on the wind by three crows.
Two more hills, time and steps slow,
eyes finally raised from stony ground.
Appreciate new growth.

A path is revealed in the wake of harvested timber.
Dog leash pulls toward it; a lighter heart follows.
Discover worn stones leading down an old boreen.

Interest is awakened, fallow deer disturbed
to float over brambles and moss-covered rocks.
Hide in the saplings to observe the intruder.

Footsteps capture the rhythm of a more contented heart.
One foot before the other.
Breathe in the wisdom of the oaks.

Eyes replete with nature, drink in the gap between
the Comeraghs and the Knockmealdowns.
Soul bathed in blackbird song.

Troubles take the perspective of distant hills,
shimmer, fade, reduce.
Solutions rise like hope on a sunny day.
Paths end, clouds break, blue sky peeks through.
Gently at first, as if scanning the horizon to ensure it is safe.

Returning home, winding down the hill to Town.
Decompression. Restored, refreshed,
ready to re-join the world anew.

Glenary Village

The stones of Glenary village are quiet,
walls that once held laughter and tears now bare,
A rusty nail, where once a picture hung.

Tables set for a tea, never eaten.
Front doorsteps still smooth,
scrubbed hard like faces for Sunday mass.

A village in mourning for its people.
Clonmel, glowed below.
Drew the young like moths to a flame.
The village stood empty as the last person left.

A stark memorial to times past.
Some walls remain, a green museum.
Ghostly village lost to progress and change.

St Mary's Chimes

A walk to Holy Year Cross.
Visiting hikers stack stones, random piles mark their way.
Brambles entwined form a lover's embrace
across the boreen to homes over fifty years deserted.

Head down against the gusting wind.
Dove grey blanket covers the hill.
Rain drooped firs await the impending shower.

Listen as heavy engines struggle through the sky above,
silence blackbird song with their deep primeval thrum.
Yellow gorse waves in the breeze,
pink trumpets raised to the humid air.

Closing blue sky framed by clouds,
giddy butterflies dance before the storm.
No-one's fool, wily sheep skip down the mountain.
They know the bare mountain
offers little shelter for the unprepared.

Take cover in the Hazel Grove,
watch raindrops ripple in deep puddles.
The shower passes on, the sun peeps through.
A rainbow bridges one valley to the next.

Start the climb through purple heather to the Cross.
In the valley St Mary's chimes sound 12 O'Clock,
mark the direction home.

Bagwell's Folly

On a Comeragh hill, stand a gathering of coppiced oaks
overlooking the River Suir.
Tiny sentinels of Bagwell's Folly since 1814.
This feels a hallowed place, ancient, serene.

Spring brings a haze of bluebells that smoother the old oak roots.
Deep green mosses carpet the scattered rocks.
The ruin of Bagwell's observatory to mark the defeat of Napoleon.
Now fallow deer hide under dappled shade
to silently graze on rough grass.

At Summer's end, the oaks drop brown and amber leaves
to coat the confusion of brambles.
The sweet scent of ripe blackberries drift over winding paths.

Grey squirrels dart amongst the branches
to gather from nature's larder.
Soon bare branches will offer little protection
from the west wind's wrath.

Heavy footsteps kick and crunch fallen leaves.
Small wellies splash through deep puddles.
Sunday walkers inhale through woollen scarves
the sour smell of decay that foretells Winter's approach.

Nestled between the cleavage of the Comeragh hills.
Driving rain on the kitchen window
frames the silhouette of Bagwell's Folly.
The kettle boils, apple and blackberry crumble in the oven.
I prepare for short Winter Days and long Winter nights.

Autumn

Basking in September Sun.
Variegated nettle leaves wilt
on cut hedges.

Lines of golden straw bales
dry on golden stalks.
Blackberries shrivel unpicked
on briars as thick as a babes' arm.

Fallen apples mush brown
into grey gravel.
Lush sodden fields
steam.

Too late summer has arrived
as school children return.
Farmers' harvests gathered.
Still. Better late than never.

Arise & Dance

Fallen leaves arise.
Dance to the rhythm of the wild wind.
Swirl through the air. Bewitch.
Bestow the gift of wonder.

Float back to inertia then inevitable decay
as the tune dies away.
Red, brown, ochre.
Lose luster, veins fading, translucent.

Become still, dormant
until the magic stirs them to dance again.
Once more lost to the rhythm of the wild wind.

All Hallows

All hallows eve.
Ghostly dancers circle the gardens of the living.

The light is soft, pockets of mist drift slowly away
from conifers on Canon Hill.
Black crows caw, sweep and dive above oaks on Bagwell's Folly.

Buzzards roost wait for the thermals.
One thousand undead walk Clonmel streets,
witches and vampires knock on unfamiliar doors.

The usual demons stalk through town.
Lying in wait to reclaim territory after Halloween has passed.
In the dawn of All Souls Day, the circle will begin again.

Homage to Winter

Dappled skeletons lift branches in homage
to the weak rays of a rare winter sun.
Ghostly, they face the cold mountain,
straining upward to embrace the warmth.

The sunlight creates prisms,
rainbows shine through the fresh raindrops
to dangle like tears from twig ends.

Along the forest path, frosted spider webs
suspended in yellow gorse.
Sparkle, a deathly hammock for the unwary.

Spiders withdraw into the shadows,
Harvest at leisure,
bounty fresh from the larder.

Relationships

Hard times -
these too shall pass.

Gilded Cage

He targets, grooms, showers honeyed words.
You look good, fawns admiration.
You're so smart, oozes adoration.
You're the one for me. Slowly ensnares,
weaves the trap. An ivory tower for the princess.

Breadcrumbs sprinkled. Carefully, nourishes need.
Don't need them. You have me.
They don't understand. Encourages separation.
We're in love. Creates distance.
We're all we need. Just us. Isolation.

Curtains cover unseen bars of a cage. Prisoner.
Temperature changes, withdraws to emotional wasteland.
You're wearing that! Distain.
Putting on weight? Enter self-doubt.
What do you know? Crushed. Self-loathing.

Tread this path alone.
Nowhere to turn. Punishment breeds confusion.
Extinguishes laughter, life, hope.

Gilded Cage, a pet to torture. Curl up, withdraw, deflect, die.
Something changes, small chink of light.
Like a flower you reach toward it.

Predator senses threat; old tricks used.
Hope lights darkness. Escape isn't easy.
Life Returning.

You are smart. You look good.
Break the chains. Escape the ivory tower.
Walk the long road, back to you.
Narcissism is a disease. No known cure.
Be strong, life is short.
Be free and don't look back.

Toad

Reclined on the lounge;
fat cheeks blown out.
Green eyes red rimmed
from late night drinking, bulged.

A toad, corpulent stomach
dominated
the view of the couch.

Poisonous words dripped
from his lips
like slime from a rock.

Vile and ugly, made so by malicious words.
Toxic waste in his veins
destroying a once good-looking youth.

Now, when she gazed on him,
she saw a toad,
Where once
she had seen a prince.

Walls

A familiar tale. The dress is bought, the hotel booked.
A fine wedding held. Family come from far and wide.
The honeymoon ensues, a palace sought.
An image in a silver frame, holds the happy couple.
The story unfolds, time and life take their toll.
Walls that should shelter, imprison.

Angels become devils.
Neighbours wear thin smiles.
Noises through thin walls.
Fairy tales are read at bedtimes that know little sleep.

Within those walls,
the Ogre arrives after closing
to sit at the end of a bed.
Eyes tight shut, breathing low.

Within those walls, neighbours listen but choose not to hear.
Gossip but not support, stay well clear.

In Parnell Street,
behind a stout door, a sanctuary lies.
Within those walls, ears listen but do not judge.
Tissues offered until tears are dried.
Within those walls,
support freely given to those in need.
Build the strength to make a stand to reveal
the fairy tale that became Grimm.

Street Angel, House Devil

Safety is a luxury, peace of mind a given.
Taken for granted as a right
for those secure in their love.
How can they offer succour when their world is whole?

Not for them, perpetual fear or anguish.
Havoc wrought by street angel,
house devil.
Stalker of the night.

Not for them mental or physical harm.
This devil of course knows
how to play the game.
Kind and polite to neighbours.

Happy people don't believe in monsters.
Spout shallow empathy based
on naive foundations of disbelief.
In many ways they do more harm than good.

They don't understand, their faces imply
Surely life cannot be so bad.
Insult to injury.
Implications of lies.

Add another nail in the prison door.
Another reason to cast down head in failure.
Let the contented pass on by,
self-righteous in their happiness.

Diplomats

Children of divorce or separation
Are born diplomats.
Why wouldn't they be?
They are a product of war.

Assets to be used strategically.
Pawns, trained on the battlefield of
Graduations, Weddings, Christmas.
Financial or emotional support can be withheld.

Allies are chosen.
Loyalties played.
Parents shamefully deploy
these weapons of mass destruction.

In turn, they learn the impartial poker face.
Take no sides. Have knowledge but none to share.
Knowledge may not always be power.
It may wreak havoc.

Don't forget they in their turn
have power. Parents should realise,
old age must be faced. These are the people
who will choose your nursing home.

After all,
they cannot have favorites in this war.
They must remain neutral
To the bitter end.

Observations and Memories

Wings

Motionless wings catch my eye,
a hawk in Winter's pale blue sky.
A sky cloudless, bitter cold.
~~*~~
Recall wings against a deep blue Mediterranean sky.
Corfu, a frappe served at the edge of a cliff.
Sold from a wooden shack selling honey.

A cliff top cafe.
Proudly the owner says, Take a seat. Enjoy the view.
Heart racing, I watch wings of seabirds, course, and dive.

Frappe finished, my heart is at peace.
Horizon blends blue sky and sea.

The owner tells me he is closing, his wife collects him,
I watch their scooter speed down the steep narrow path.
The couple are 70 year's young, he clings to her,
her grey hair blows wild in the breeze.

~~*~~
At the beach, my children have shocking news.
And she was really old, they say.
She took off her dress and put on her hat.
Just the hat, they tell me wide eyed.
In the distance, her skinny silhouette framed in the brim of her hat.
Naked as the day she was born.

~~*~~
Blue Corfu, the island
where age is a number not a condition.
Where the magic of sunset renews happiness.
Where a wide brimmed hat could be all you need
to give you wings.

Bambi

We all have those friends.
You know the ones. Bambi.
Even when it's about you, it's about them.
Somehow the focus moves the spotlight squarely back to them.

Lately, patience wears thin.
Temper locked and loaded.
Stay of execution, hold fire.
Words that would kill the friendship,
held back. New boundaries drawn.

Avoid the pity party.
Ignore the Bambi eyes.
The relentless search for sympathy.
Place to lay blame.

Temper barely held ignites.
Stoke up the BBQ
for venison. Safety catch applied.
Beware Bambi, one more word,
And it's open season.

Isolation

Isolation. Away from the busy world.
Stay at home. Keep your world small.
Protect yourself and others. Stay at home.
Where these words a death knell or a freedom cry?

Time slowed, dragged, flew.
You listened to bird song and not traffic. It lifted you.
Or listened to the news, worried about the numbers.
It took you down.

Did you do all you planned?
Did yoga stretch your mind and body.
Was there enough time? Did you want more?

Were you prepared? Did you paint, colour your world.
Garden for the bees. Save the planet.
Or worry that your cupboards were bare.
Did you crave the usual food or explore new menus?

Do you relish being alone or does solitude not suit you?
Did you feel trapped or free; or at times both?
There were lessons to be learned.
Did you learn them, or will you forget?

This time is a gift.
The clock ticks to the beat of your resting heart.
Or when the clocks tick more quickly,
will you relish what you missed.

When the rain cleared and the sun shone through the window,
did you see hope
or dirt?

Your own monastery protected from unhappy retail therapy.
Or did you order online. Hands sore from scrolling.
Did you enjoy your isolation?
free from entering the world?

At last free to work from home,
or spend time in your own hotel.
Staycation or prison, it's a state of mind.
Life is what you make of it.

When you walked, did you see you own local world?
Did you worry that the fox is treading quieter paths?
Straying into human domain.
Facing danger when this time passes.

Would you retreat again to the quietness of solitude.
Did you heal?
Salve your regrets, walk down old paths.
Did you heal and become joyful once again?

Isolate.
Time for you to reflect,
did you like who you met?

This Time

This time reveals the glory of the introvert
who revels in isolation and the extrovert
who struggles away from the crowd.

This time reveals acquaintances who become friends;
Friends who drift to become acquaintances.
School friends reminisce ancient deeds.
Family photos of shared history.

This time, your gift of reflection.
A personal stocktake.
Examine the importance of self-reliance.
Build inner strength, resilience.

Clear away mental and physical clutter.
This time allows peace.
Gain knowledge of true friends, the kindness of strangers.
A time to heal through reflection.

Remember Me

Wedged like a house spider between
the doors of O'Neill's public bar and funeral parlour,
the canvassing politician feasts on the bones of misfortune.
So sorry for your loss.... (brief pause),
Can I rely on your support?

Ever vigilant for new mourners,
clumsy eagerness, consolation dripping from an insincere tongue.
Feigned pity resting briefly in the eye.
A hunter, the unburied, the bait in the web.

A prime location providing an endless supply
of potential support.
Left to right glances, so sorry for your loss.
Remember me in the election.

Not to be thwarted, appears again at the doors of the church.
Hands must be shaken, opportunity seized.
The coffin followed, five abreast in step with the voters.
A man of the people, ready to partake of the funeral plate.

Pity the poor corpse, whose politics may differ.
Suspended ready for the grave,
gone from being dogged at the doorstep
by pension seeking politicians, lowered to eternity
to the tune of the words

Remember me in the election....
Can I rely on your support?

Flymo Walk

Park in Upper Glenary.
Just at the limit of my 2k COVID walk.
Walk up the stony hill, past the stream that gushed
now trickles, thanks to hot April sunny days.

Fork left past the harvested timber; pine resin heavy in the air.
Gorse bushes compete adding coconut.
Assault on the senses.
Vibrant yellow on deep moss green.

Fork right climb the gentle hill.
Bird song serenade.
Miles of countryside in every direction.
A flymo lawnmower abandoned.
I wonder was the job too big or the cable too short?

Onward to the top, fork right onto primrose path.
A carpet of soft yellow, dotted with buttercups,
shy violets and primroses.
Fork right, down the steep hill.

Spot the COVID Rebel.
An older man with seven decades under his hat
pushes his racing bike up the hill. Smile sympathetically.
He laughs, "Broke the wheel, flying down the last hill."
A lesson. My sympathies were due only for his plight.

Wind down the bend.
Nearing the end of what I now call, flymo walk.
I slow my pace to allow a proud pheasant stroll across the road.
After all, life is good. There is no rush.

Goddess of Spring

Persephone slumbers beneath velvet skies,
Returning to Earth to bring Spring.
Captive.
She dreams of Hades.
Her love.

In perpetual Winter, he dwells.
Wine flows through her veins,
Like the Styx through the underworld.

Summoned by his grief,
She drifts to him in dreams.
The candlelight, a flickering sentinel,
Throws a warm glow to draw her back.

She endures warm sunshine,
Until Winters frost signals her return.
Once again safe in his embrace.

It's a Waste

You can't take it with you when you're gone.
To clarify, this means when you are dead,
not on a day out.

And not, the coffee cup you queued up for
but cannot manage to carry home.
Dumped on a stone bridge over a sparkling stream.

Or the sofa bought on 24 months credit.
Barely paid for when
your style palate changed.
Tipped out of a van in the woods.
Returned to nature, who tries to smoother it.
Blend to green.

A wardrobe of clothes still sporting labels.
Bagged for Thursday's charity collection.
Brush shoulders with the post man
carrying parcels from China or India.
Sweatshops that made the dress,
Made Just for You.

A thousand years to break down
the items you owned for a heartbeat.
These will never return
to nature.

Only Playing

My hearing is crap.
My distance eyesight dim.
My polite request for you to leash your dogs
Is either unheard or unheeded.

My knees have been grazed,
My arms stretched long at the end of leads,
My back twisted to the tune of
"It's alright, he's only playing".

My Walk to escape drama
Has inflicted yours on me.
I watch two long tongues loll over
Large canine incisors.

I wonder if I should let my dogs
Play too.
You may not sound so cheerful then.

Muddy Paws

The agony of Winter's muddy floors.

The futility of achieving clean,
only for the backdoor to open.

To admit muddy paws.

Omelette for Lunch

18 free range eggs delivered to my door.
Run home, omelette for lunch.
Carefully lift box.

Box floor drops.
Rapidly clutch to chest,
10 eggs rise and fall broken.
Squawk.

Sprint across floor, drip eggy trail.
Trip across mat, four more, crack.
Yellow yolks surf high on white tidal wave.
Recede. Cracked shells float forlornly.

Save four, whole.
Rescue four cracked.
Whisk. Season. Cook.
Tip rest to dog bowls.

Sponge trail of woe.
Still.
Omelette for lunch. Relax.
Then wonder if dogs can eat too many eggs?

Congratulations on your Graduation

From the first plaintive wail to the graduation robe, a parent is doomed to fail more often than succeed.

Mother Nature must have given the job of food to Father Nature.
Who else would think sensitive bits go into something with iron gums,
certainty of teeth and very possibly fangs.

From the Mother in Law's cynical frown to the visiting nurse's scales.
Judgement will be passed, too light or too heavy.
Implied inadequacy conveyed.
Judged against the babies, who eat like a grown man or are sound sleepers.
To the sympathetic tired grin from the night-time driver,
whose keys in the door wake a wailer to walk the floor.

From Teachers good and bad, role models who know more than you.
It really is a wonder you made it this far.
The gnashing of teeth in parties given, children entertained.
Or the parties missed, not part of the cool gang.
Multiple Barbies and Lego, and wishing money was an acceptable gift.
To entertaining their friends you love, the friends you don't.

To the inevitability of a mobile phone, censored like another child.
Joining clubs, going on day trips, taking grinds.
Doing their projects and only getting a B.

Collections and drop offs, being early, embarrassing or late and neglectful.
The dramas on and off stage, from wanting you to listen to their woes
to defending their rights.
Teenagers who wear a path from the bedroom to the fridge.
Squabble over front seats of the car and control of the stereo.

On to college, standing on their own two feet.
While trekking home with washing then dragging back shopping.

To a time when you may have learned a thing or two.
You may have stumbled often but you eventually passed.
This is a time to recover, draw breath before the next phase begins.
Congratulations on your graduation.

Unigate Girl

The milk float pulls in
2 full cream for number 19.
The milkman smiles and waves as
you hop on to hitch a lift down the hill.

Stilettos dangle from crimson nails,
long calves swing slim ankles back and forth
to the gentle hum of the milk float.
Front gardens of red and pink roses pass slowly by.

Bottles clink. Some empty, some full.
Ready for the doorsteps.
The red foil top glistens,
Rainbow sparkles in the early morning sun.

Bottles slippery with dew,
Grabbed with a wink for the morning cuppa.
Ready for the day.
Stilettos rest by the front door until the next time.

True Friends

A true friend would tell you
If your skirt is tucked into your knickers.
Or if there is lipstick on your teeth.

A true friend would tell you
How it is
And how it could be.

A true friend will tell you
What you need to know
And you will still be friends.

Everyone needs one true friend.
Consider yourself lucky
If you have one.

Peace at Last

At last, my head has become a quiet space.
Heart at rest, beats gently.
Inside the torch of perpetual anger, dampened, smoulders.
Words now committed to the page.

Demons that stalked my soul at night,
dug trenches to furrow my brows.
Anxiety etched deeply across my face.
Redundant, now at rest.

Jaws are still, I do not grind my teeth
to rubble to loosen my metal fillings.
These pages, a grave for the fear of ages.
This book a doorway to pass through to the future.

Kind Words for this book

This collection of poems, by Theresa Jones, will inspire you with its honesty and resilience. Theresa's sense of irony hits top notes that will resonate and reverberate. Her unmistakable voice and it's love of nature and people makes this collection, like herself, a unique gift to be treasured.

Eileen Acheson,
author of "I Wonder"

About the Author

I am originally from London, England.
I have two wonderful children.
I live near the beautiful Comeragh Mountains, Ireland.
Apart from working most of the week,
I spend time walking my dogs, hacking out on Buster and writing.

I was inspired to write poetry after taking part in a library workshop with Margaret Galvin. I never realized that I could write poetry until I tried.

Writing has opened worlds to let me take part in
Spoken Word events in local festivals
such as Clonmel Junction Festival, Applefest; and
the Clancy Festival with writers of Poetry Plus through Margaret O'Brien
and Linda Fahey of Tudor Artisan Hub -
exciting collaborations with writers, artists and musicians on projects
such as
screenwriting project on the Culture Night film "*If Anyone Asks*",
song writing "*Stay Strong* (with Mia Carney and Marie Walsh).

These are opportunities that I had never thought
would be available to a South London girl.

Printed in Poland
by Amazon Fulfillment
Poland Sp. z o.o., Wrocław

65249854R00045